Starving in a Chrysalis

Starving in a Chrysalis

Poetry by
Ashley Eikenberry

STARVING IN A CHRYSALIS
All rights reserved
Copyright © 2023 by ASHLEY EIKENBERRY
Cover art copyright © 2023 by ASHLEY EIKENBERRY

ISBN: 979-8-218-26887-9

No part of this publication may be reproduced, stored in a retrieval system, or transmitted in any form or by any means electronic, mechanical, photocopying, recording, or otherwise, without the written permission of the author or publisher.

For little me and little you.

To all who have ever wandered without a voice.

Contents

Author's Note 1

Birthing 3
    Not All Caterpillars Fly 4
    Becoming 5
    Hummingbird 6
    Buried 7
    No Ground 8
    Tree 9
    Home 10
    Cradle 11
    The Seed 12
    Belly of the Bird 13
    Teacher 14
    Forever in Bloom 15
    First Signs of Spring 16
    Roots Undone 17
    Early Dawn 18

Breathing 19
    Intuition 20
    Love letter 21
    Sleep 22
    Presence 23
    Driftwood 24
    Tide 25
    God 26
    Liberate 27
    Be 28
    Joy 29
    Gratitude 30
    Spanish Moss 31
    Glory 32
    2022 33
    The Bottom 34
    Feeling 35

Emerging 37

- Leaf Shadows 38
- Guide 39
- Wind Chimes 40
- The Will of a Wildflower 41
- Glisten 42
- Watercolor the Soul 43
- Sun and Moon 44
- Liminal Space 45
- Time 46
- Reweave 47
- Care 48
- Essence 49
- As Above So Below 50
- The Familiar Ache 51
- Changing Sides 52
- A Desert Sunset 53

Reparenting 55

- The Great Mother 56
- The Web 57
- Grandmother Spider 58
- Honor the Orphan 59
- Hands 60
- Hawk 61
- Dear exile 62
- The Medial Woman 64
- Renewal 66
- Tangled 68
- Alligator 69
- Unity 70
- Teenager 72
- Dripping with Children 74
- Ouroboros 75

In the end - A special dedication 76

- We Belong to Her 76

Author's Note

As a highly sensitive person, I have felt the world as a poem for as long as I can remember. I never considered myself a writer. I've felt an acute sense of shame and have been teased about spelling all my life. In early childhood, I experienced times of chaos and insecurity. In second grade, a teacher noticed that I had trouble seeing. My whole world was fuzzy, and I had adopted this as "normal." The day I finally got glasses, I awoke to an incredibly intricate and beautiful world. I remember seeing a tree, A TREE! They were magnificent.

The glasses didn't cure everything though. I always had a restless and struggling part of me, and from an early age, I began trying on different personas, so as to become the person I was convinced I needed to be. This caused me much internal pain. I spent many of my childhood and adult years saying yes when I meant no, only to survive, and I lost myself.

On August 20th, 2013, I arrived at the seat of sobriety, and since then, I've been on a journey committed to my inner world and seeking wholeness.

It was, perhaps, being unable to see clearly that cultivated this highly sensitive part of me. For so long, my emotions were lost at sea. Around the time that I started this book, they flooded through me. During the Summer of 2021, my husband, child, and I unexpectedly moved from the Midwest, where I had lived in a shelter of familiarity, to the deep, muggy, and steamy South. There, I once again landed in the depths of loneliness. I now understand it as a chrysalis. During this time, most of the poems in this book started to pour out of me, and I embraced this deep and emotional journey by birthing this book.

These poems are about transformation, growing up, and learning to reparent myself through nature. Because I now know I am, and always have been, held by the Earth.

Birthing

Not All Caterpillars Fly

Who is fond of the in between
A cocoon of unknowing
Riddled with illusions from many directions
A profound heartache
An unrealistic need
Longing
Churning
Starving in a chrysalis
Not all caterpillars fly

Becoming

One day I decided I was a poet

And all the thoughts and feelings swirling

Transformed into words from all the yearning

Hummingbird

Birthing a book from the heart
Looks a lot like a hummingbird flying still

The flutter of beats from inside my chest

Going, going, going

Gone

Buried

Roots don't grow by being tied down
Instead
They have to be buried

No Ground

In the muggy south
There is no ground
The oak trees roots
Are all I've found

Tree

There will never be
A presence more free
Then sitting with the solace of a tree

Grounding from the sea
The emotional part of me

Belongs high above the breeze
In ease

Home

A home is only the ego
If you're attached to it

Cradle

Winter is a womb
Cradle it

Treat it like a holy tomb

Honor what you will leave behind
With stillness, images, and emotions

We are both dead and alive
Nonexistent without the other

Like the bulbs deep in the frozen ground
We never know what will bloom
This time around

The Seed

What if everything I need
Is a seed
That is already planted
What if I trust myself entirely

Belly of the Bird

In the belly of the bird
Lies a song to be heard

Nothing makes me feel more superb
Then what's in the belly of the bird
Awaiting every morning to be heard

Like the moons time
The bird needs no alarm
To keep time, aligned

And here I sit every morning in awe
Of the magnificent order, of it all

Teacher

Nothing is more resilient
Than a tree that blooms too soon
Let her be your teacher

Forever in Bloom

Marveling that creator brought me to this place

The place where blooming is year-round

Where unfolding is always in process

And abundance is a steady flow

Like my wild and open heart

Maybe it's a dream

First Signs of Spring

Let yourself sense

The gospel of the birdsong
The spirit of a wildflower
The strength of an oak tree
The flow of a creek bed
The ooze of mud between your toes
The power of a rainstorm
The whisper of the wind

Breathe in the pigments and aroma of the first signs of spring

Give gratitude to the sun
The soul of Earth's mystery

Roots Undone

For years I spent living untapped from the root
A lost, little seedling who longed to take foot

Swimming in cavernous springs from below
The oceans, they crashed into the shore under my toe

The emotions, they gripped me

Feeling so low

To ground is a choice
For some
They may say

For others
Deeply connected to nature
Surrendering is only
To the seasons at play

Early Dawn

No early dawn will ever be
As neat as when the barred owls came to me

A spring of change
Horizon new

Yet every morning they were there
Felt in view

They called to each other from the hollow oaks
Sweeping down
Their wings like cloaks
Hunting for owlets
Is no joke

I beamed with light before their moon like eyes
Everyday I felt more surprise

Until the day we migrated together

Because in life we don't get to feel that special
For forever

Breathing

Intuition

Intuition fascinates me

The ability to listen from inside ourselves is an instinctual form of integrity

It likely begins in the body

A rumble of the belly
A thumping of the heart
A fullness in the throat

Or a strong and long intake of breath

Truth bumps

To find our way,
We will likely start by finding our way

Back to our bodies

Notice

Inside

Love letter

This morning my heart wrote a love letter to my mind

And in that moment

I was able to unwind

Sleep

Cry yourself to sleep
Do so without releasing a peep
Inward spirals
Watch them go
Wishing you could go deep
Into the world of dreams
A land where messages and symbols hold your hand
The final freedom
Fairyland

Presence

Do you experience awe and wonder
For me, it's the coolness of a deep inhale in the pine forest
A symphony of birdsong
Spotting a red-headed woodpecker
Somatically experiencing the whisper of the wind
Watching a caterpillar move through the world
Even a moist dog nose sticky with blades of fresh grass
A grounding we often take for granted
Available to all who are willing to pay attention

Driftwood

Have you ever wondered what it would be like to be
Driftwood

Where would you want to wash ashore

The beautiful masterpiece taught me an incredible lesson

Spending several minutes caressing the layers of this
washed-up loblolly pine tree

Wondering what all she had to be
Wondering if she could feel the touch of me

What if we honored all of Earth's creatures
Even as they decay

Trees, our ancestors, have long provided our species
with food, shelter, protection, and breath

What if we took time to contemplate the life of a tree
Our remarkable symbiotic relationship

What if, like the layers of bark
We, too, have layers that attach to the human heart

Tide

A longing to feel
Gently
As the waves flip against the shore in a peaceful low tide

In and out
Like the breath
Inhale
Pause
Exhale

A rip tide is not sustainable
It's violent and distorted
It causes havoc on the beach

And the breath
Even the body

Yet, it can't be avoided

They say feelings aren't facts
Yet, what happens somatically is real

A longing in between

To feel experience
Without fear

Wrapped in a steady security
Like my favorite blanket in the beachy breeze

God

God is of me
But cannot be contained
In me

Outside
Inside

I won't decide
Where God resides

Below
Above
Beside

I will not hide
Faith won't subside
I'll stay wide-eyed
And keep an open mind

Liberate

I try
too hard
To change the unchangeable
To accept the unacceptable

Be

Can you just

Be

Without the need for attachments

Without the desire to question

Let the past

Go

So

The present can just

Be

Joy

Joy is a butterfly dancing in your path

Gratitude

Gratitude is to the mind
What oxygen is to the lung

Spanish Moss

Spanish moss is like a tear
Joy or sorrow
Depending on the weather

Glory

Have you ever sung a lullaby to a mountain
Or watched a yellow swallowtail dance
Swearing that this one
For sure
Has to be a fairy

Or spent a humid, sticky, sunny day
Submerged in a freezing, spring-fed creek

So glorious you finally understand baptism

2022

Hope is not a replacement
For fear
But a companion
To hold dear

Sometimes I dream
I'm a rock
Deep down at the bottom of a river
Where the air is gone
And my soul is cold and calm
No longer needing to regulate my breathing

When I no longer feel alive in this so-called scheme

The Bottom

Feeling

One day soon will be the last
I'll walk this old familiar path

The feeling hit me like a grasp
In that moment left aghast

The thought of this took my breath away

Like the time I fell backward off a swing
hitting the cold, hard, frozen ground with a thud

Memories of the first time I felt the wind knocked right out of me

Learning I can let this feeling be
While still navigating, its intensity

Emerging

Leaf Shadows

My mind wonders like dancing leaf shadows on a clear and windy day

Yet the more I sit and watch the dancing shadows

The more my mind stands still

Guide

Amygdala tending
In the depths of surrendering

Every end has a beginning
Every sunset
A sunrise

Nature will always be my guide
My muse
My ground
Sacred solace
To restore my sound

Held in the breast of the clouds
An endless heartbeat knows no bounds

Wind Chimes

Flutters like the wind chimes of my heart
The breeze blows hard and fast
And through the mind in whispers
I call upon the roots to keep me steady
Ideas and dreams come pouring in
To which direction, there is no end

Seemingly at a crossroads
She came to me for a reason
Forever changing, is my internal season

One can only pause for so long
Before one will be moved to a decision

The Will of a Wildflower

Contemplating the will of a wildflower
What are the conditions needed to grow

Being versus doing
A balance of nature and resiliency

All thoughts back to the sun

Does a wildflower have a will

I live with the brain of a human
And the heart of a wildflower

Glisten

You never truly know the meaning of glisten
Until you see it through the eyes of the morning sun

Watercolor the Soul

How do you show up for the sunrise of the soul

As if each day you were painting a watercolor version of the sky

What if you could choose the colors of your masterpiece

Would it include ultramarine blue or burnt umber

Have you ever watercolored a sky

If all you're experiencing is pain, exhaustion, and overwhelm

You've forgotten you have a divine right, a grace period, a pause, a surrender

Rest easy

You've forgotten you're here to experience pleasure, joy, and gratitude

What colors do you choose for your soul

Sun and Moon

There is a special time of the morning
To commune with the sun and the moon

How often are you present for the first bird song

Liminal Space

Forever in a liminal space

Existing in the places in between

Finding comfort in waiting

Honoring the Divine instead of willing the way

Swimming around the threshold

Learning to relax and float

Trusting

Caretaking the soul

Swinging with decisions

Wide open

Time

For what seemed like forever
My favorite time of the year was Fall

It is now
I realize
Of course it was

After it all
It's impossible to know until you do

What it's like to bloom in midlife

My favorite time of year is Spring

Reweave

Finding the gold
and
Finding the darkness

Are both necessary to reweave the personality

Care

Strive for life with contentment and meaning

Experience beauty that isn't owned

Find wholeness in others
Through a universal center that's radiating in you

Care for yourself seriously
And for others the same

Essence

The brief moment when you realize your insides match your outsides

You're living today in a way that's true to you

You know your essence

You're open to the powerful Godesss within you

You know if want peace, you have to be peace

Or when you want adventure, you have to wander

If you crave boundaries, you have to lean into anger and even embrace your rage

And when you want awe, celebrate the beauty that radiates from within you

As Above So Below

If great birds of prey are metaphors
for higher consciousness

Then let the vast power of their shadow
on a mountainside remind you of the unconscious

For as above
so below

The Familiar Ache

It's settling in
An aching, longing, for the familiar

When I stepped out for my walk today
The first feeling took my breath away

Craving adventure
Has never been greater than built security

Even if it's a false sense
There will always be things that I miss

Changing Sides

Perception is the great divide
Everyone is experiencing the same sunset

Most have lost touch to the illusion
A jig of misconstrue

Individuate from the collective
Non-normative satisfaction

Like the blissful cadence of a dragonfly
Make time to dance with the sun

The soul feeds on its environment
A truth not to be persuaded

A Desert Sunset

When time solely becomes awe

Reparenting

The Great Mother

The great mother doesn't walk into rooms wondering what other people need, or what they are thinking

She walks in attuned to her emotional and spiritual needs

And they are met

She is at home within herself

She is safe

She is secure

Her cadence as regulated as her nervous system

The body is her anchor

She is grounded in a truth she couldn't know until now

She knows she is enough

She's traded pain and exhaustion for pleasure and tenderness

And in humility, she is at peace

The Web

Like a spider
I'm forever webbing my way

Grandmother Spider

Grandmother spider
Waiting in her web

Weaving out the mysteries
Dancing through my head

Unmoved by the croaking crow
Or the scattered squirrel

So still in her wisdom

Observing the miracle of life

Willing to lend out a mother

Honor the Orphan

Come in, my dear, sit close
Don't fear my long black cloak
You have been scurrying for so long
The time has come
Sit here with me

You see there is nothing to fear
My dear

You no longer must suffer
You no longer must grit your teeth and hold on tight

Relax easy into the flow
The water is running
Rest in the float
You are carried
You are heard
I am hear to listen
To keep your words and treat them as though they are sacred

You will not be judged
You will only be journeyed
Back
Home

Hands

Her stories are my stories
Our stories are one

My grams hands

Hawk

When I found you dead
I finally knew

It was time to let go
Of the raptor boundaries

That helped me to grow

Whole

Dear exile

Dear exile,
How do I get to you

The greatest philosophers and analysts of all time have the words
The words have helped me know you
But yet I have never met you

From the cold, dark shadows of my mind, you lure
For years
I have met you in my dreams and my active imagination

But have I felt you

To know is different than to feel
To feel you is on the edge of impossible
Vulnerability as such was cut with the umbilical cord
Uprooted, evicted, banished

Becoming, longing, learning how to be there for you

It is my highest calling and obligation not to give up

To sit and sift in the shadows
Until you emerge

In my body, not my intellect
Naked, lost, and even terrified

Maybe in each deep breath
In each moment of quiet devotion to you

Finally, you will feel safe enough to merge

Not as a complex
But as a beloved part

I am here
I am unsteady
But I vow
I am ready

The Medial Woman

To walk the path of the medial woman

One may experience beauty and humility in karmic mirrors

Awe-inspiring wonder

A chthonic hearer

Presence that takes the breath away

Ancestors of trees and stones and rivers

Animal intuition

Oneness most humans ignore

Not heard by modern language

Liminal open spaces

Inner home in an outer world

Footprints walking towards unlearning

Feeling unknowable places

A tender creative spark, forever ignited

In spite of being invited

A sidereal alliance

Brought on by a choice we may not always remember

Whether it's July or December

Our rites engender

Compassion, nourishment, and abundant love

The path of a lantern in the night

Able to see in the dark

Renewal

In order to be renewed, we must feel through the darkness

One does not walk in the light without sifting through the cloudy troubles of the past

Past must be revealed
Parts unveiled

Remember you were born for this

You were born as perfect Love

Everyone here on Earth earns a swampy soul
Curing old wounds, sharing with others, feeling into old stories
Assists the collective in healing

Like the hawk perched up in the tree outside my window

You too can watch from above
The higher consciousness the hawk possesses is in you

You can separate the truth from the false
You were born free
You were born true

You have the power of rebirth
Renew it all
Just be

Give yourself space to allow the deep winter foggy
haze to fall away

Time holds, gentle time

Your voice will come
Let it come naturally

Be devoted
Pay attention

You know right where you are, is right where you are

Tangled

I showed up in this incarnation
Tangled

Although my body was pure and new
My soul was rather worn

A tangled ball of yarn

I'm tangled in me, my life, my childhood

I'm tangled in you, your life, your childhood

Childhood marks our initiations and exposures to karma from this lifetime and the last

Childhood is where we are rather powerless over what happens to our balls of yarn

Perhaps I'll spend my whole life untangling

My only hope is I can worry about my own yarn enough and stay out of your tangle

But karma tangles our yarn together from this lifetime and the last

Instead of feeling hopeless, maybe I'll stay curious

Maybe I'll remind myself that even a tangle is connection

Alligator

Alligator came to me as road kill

Served by the sages of the south

Served on what I now know was a silver platter

Who would have thought this was my first experience being mothered

Unity

A journey
A spiritual continuum of discernment
A shift in perception
An integration of a wounded part

I'm learning that forgiveness is so I don't have to carry your darkness inside of me anymore

I used to not be able to say that word

Forgiveness

I thought it meant it was ok
what happened

I thought it meant I lost that part of me

But really it stayed tucked away

Then I learned a little grace
She was fierce
Grace lays hold of time
She demands inconvenience
And works closely with her sister grief

I found compassion in lieu of forgiveness
Inside of me I found a Self
Deep, deep within
So far inside of me
Once exiled

It is in an unveiling
A ritual so sacred

It is in the expression of her
Of me
That I can love you

And in the mingling of our parts

That I can see me
In you

And you
In me

Both longing

Only to be
In unity

Teenager

Four thousand words later
My soul remembers

It's my experience, strength, and hope
That keeps me afloat

Adolescence isn't a curse
It's where we pick up the pieces and place them in our psychological purse

Before we understand being understood

Where longing is belonging

And our bodies become new

When we give up caring for social status

And confuse being a muse in the biopsychosocial stratus

Where sometimes it's all we have to hang on

To amuse those caregivers
Who just never stop caring about...

Everything

Stay true to the authentic parts
Despite the fawning around you
In spite of the fawning around you

Keep making art

Your identity matters

Even when you feel lost
Don't give up no matter the cost

Dripping with Children

In the heart of all my healing
I was holding so many tender parts of me
I began to be dripping with children

Longing for acceptance of my childish ways
I abruptly recognized
It was always, and only through her
That a way of my own could be paved

At first, I became her
Raw, vulnerable, hyper, but still
Unable to accept safety in the world
Belonging to no one and everyone at once
Confused and conflicted
So much I won't mention

Then, I held her
And shared her
In order to meld her

Until one day, I was mature enough to know
To love myself whole
I had to let a part of her go

And that's when acknowledging the little hero inside of me
Became enough to set me free

Ouroboros

Inside the chambers of the eternal heart

Is home to the only true mother
And the space of the inner little ones

Born of dirt and sea
Only ever of me

Like a movie screen
I continue to dream
Waking up I scream
No longer unseen

From the cavernous earth of underground rivers

Through fault lines

Arriving to unerring elevations

When rooting becomes rooted
And attachment becomes detached

Where the linear
Spirals
Back in itself

Like blood coils through the veins
Back to the beating
Flowing and fleeting

Only ever of thee
Made an ouroboros of me

In the end
A special dedication

We Belong to Her

Arriving here
I'd have told you of my knowledge of the river

Arriving here
I have so much to learn about the river

The soul of the river
Is an art form that will make you quiver
With death stories that will make you shiver

I was asked if I wanted to float the river
Not yet, I say
We're still getting to know each other

We have so much in common
But I need to earn her respect
She will let me know when I am ready

Humans believe nature belongs to them
We belong to nature

Fires, floods, storms, and heat
She is roaring

Collectively, we've replaced beauty and awe
with technology and trash

It takes courage to connect with her
And when I deeply do
The grief is almost unbearable

All dis ease stems from failure to put Earth first
A river of understanding
Does nothing for the ego

Anima mundi
Purusha
These concepts are lost to most

A species
so consumed with self
so disconnected from our animal hearts
so willing to forget we are made of blood rivers

An End.

Please accept my deepest gratitude for taking the time to hear and support me by reading Starving in a Chrysalis

Printed in the USA
CPSIA information can be obtained
at www.ICGtesting.com
LVHW041539271023
762201LV00014B/1934